Joyfully,

A Book of Devotions

JOYCE

Joyfully,
A Book of Devotions
JOYCE

Joyce Clasen

Outskirts Press, Inc.
Denver, Colorado

Joyfully, Joyce
A Book of Devotions
All Rights Reserved.
Copyright © 2009 Joyce Clasen
v3.0

Outskirts Press, Inc.
http://www.outskirtspress.com

ISBN: 978-1-4327-3560-9

Outskirts Press and the "OP" logo are trademarks belonging to Outskirts Press, Inc.

PRINTED IN THE UNITED STATES OF AMERICA

God's Abilities

God has not given us a spirit of fear,
but of power and of love and of a sound mind.
II Timothy 1:7

Now is the time to accept what God has given and rest in Him. This is an integral part of who you are in His service. You need to focus again on what you have already received from God. He has given freely of His Spirit and filled you with His power and love and a sound mind. It is God's ability and your <u>availability</u>.

I can do all things through Christ who strengthens me. Philippians 4:13

This is a statement of fact by Paul, not a wish or a desire, but a focus on the presence of God who leads and directs your life. Furthermore,

> It is God who works in you both to will and to do for His good pleasure. Philippians 2:13 (a paraphrase of this is: it is God who gives you the desire, and then He also gives you the ability to accomplish the work! TLB)

This is part of the intimate love relationship that God desires with you that Henry T. Blackaby speaks of in his book, <u>Experiencing God</u>. Your whole journey is about participating in a relationship with God, hearing His voice, listening for His direction, seeing your world through His eyes, looking to see where He is working and join Him.

You can do this daily, moment by moment: through the Word, through prayer, through fellowship and worship.

> The Lord is my rock and my fortress and my deliverer, my God my strength in whom I will trust; my shield and the horn of my salvation, my stronghold. Psalm 18:2

Often remind yourself, "it's not about me!" Esther was told: Yet who knows whether you have come to the kingdom for such a time as this? Esther 4:14

And this is true for you, too. Focus on your mission. Willingly share Him with others.

Joyfully, Joyce

God's Supply

2

My God shall supply all your need
According to His riches in glory
By Christ Jesus
Philippians 4: 19

How rich is God? What are His resources? Praise God you can draw from the well of God's wealth and not your own. The statement of fact here is that God shall supply all your need. Claim it. Ask for it. Expect it!

As this passage is written in <u>The Message:</u> "You can be sure that God will take care of everything you need, his generosity exceeding even yours in the glory that pours from Jesus."

Truly, God has an abundance to give: not only for your physical needs, but also spiritual, emotional, social and financial. What a joy when you see your needs being met in unexpected and supernatural ways. Then you can give God the glory for His supply.

It is good that you are depending on the Father, seeking His face, expecting His supply. Your situation requires it. Sure, it may come in the mail, or by new friends, or a kindness shown, but it is God who has provided.

May the Father continue to bless you in unexpected and surprising ways, from the spring of living water that never runs dry.

Through the Lord's mercies we are not consumed,
Because His compassions fail not.
They are new every morning.
Great is Your faithfulness.
"The Lord is my portion," says my soul,
Therefore I hope in Him.
Lamentations 3:22-24

Joyfully, Joyce

Hearing God's Voice

3

For we know that all things work together for good to them that love God, to them that are the called according to His purpose. Romans 8:28

How precious it is to know that God can and will speak to you in the midst of challenging circumstances. In fact, He delights to share endless truths with you when you are quiet before Him.

Be open to experiencing God, but realize that God may choose to interrupt your life. God asks you to adjust your life to Him and release your life to Him. Then He can use you. Every experience is part of God's divine Plan in developing your character for ministry. God is building relationship with you in the lean times. God is calling you to yield up to Him the crises in your life. He asks that you accept that in His love and with His knowledge you go through these times. He is there with you.

> I beseech you, brethren, by the mercies of God that you present your bodies a living sacrifice, holy and acceptable unto God, which is your reasonable service. And be not conformed to this world, but be transformed by the renewing of your mind, that you may prove what is that good and acceptable will of God. Romans 12: 1, 2

> I call heaven and earth as witnesses
> today against you, that I have set before you
> Life and death
> Blessing and cursing;
> Therefore choose life,
> that you and your descendants may live;
> That you may
>   Love the Lord your God
> That you may
>   Obey His voice
> And that you may
>   Cling to Him,

FOR HE IS YOUR LIFE... Deuteronomy
30: 19-20

<u>Now choose life, for He is your life!</u>

Joyfully, Joyce

Spending Time With God

4

There are verses that speak of God's special love for you:

The Lord appeared to us in the past saying:
> I have loved you with an everlasting love;
> I have drawn you with loving-kindness.
> Jeremiah 31:3

> How precious also are your thoughts to me,
> O God!
> How great is the sum of them. Psalm
> 139:17

> God loves you!
> God chooses you!

God calls you!
God reveals Himself to you!

God wants you to be aware of His presence, to live in His presence. Your being <u>with</u> him is of much more value than any of the things you may be doing <u>for</u> him. Henry Blackaby states: "The constant presence of God is the most practical part of your life and ministry."

Each week, plan a special time alone with God. Take time to share an outing with Him – in a garden, a park, by a lake. View a sunrise or sunset. Make it private and personal with Him. Focus on Him. Feel His love for you. Praise Him. Thank Him. Worship Him.

The God of the universe looks forward to spending time with you. God sees you as special, anointed, beloved, precious in His sight. He is calling you to enjoy His presence.

> Be still and know that I am God. Psalm 46:
> 10
> In Him we live and move and have our being. Acts 17:28

May this be your prayer: Lord, thank You for the privilege of spending time with You. Thank You for loving me unconditionally. Help me to enjoy your presence. Give me a sense of the quietness and peace that You have in store for me. Love, and amen.

Joyfully, Joyce

Knowing God

5

God chooses to reveal Himself to you through various names given in the Bible. The names for God identify His character, His nature, and something unique about His interaction with you. The names for God also reveal how you come to know Him personally through your experience.

When Moses went to the burning bush, God told Moses His name: "I AM WHO I AM." Exodus 3:14 This name was to be presented to the Israelites. God is Eternal. Moses learned more about God when there was a battle and Moses' arms were held up through the battle for victory. He experienced God as "The Lord is My Banner," Exodus 17:8-15. Abraham, in preparing to offer up Isaac on the mountain, came to know God as "My Provider - Jehovah-Jirah!" God provided a ram for the sacrifice, Genesis 22:1-18.

Henry Blackaby states in his book, <u>Experiencing God</u>: "You will never be satisfied to know about God. Knowing God only comes through experience as He <u>reveals</u> Himself to you. We get to know God and His nature personally through our experiences."

How has God revealed Himself to you recently? David, in Psalms, wrote: He is my:

Comforter	Foundation	Salvation
Counselor	Fortress	Stronghold
Deliverer	Strength	Confidence
Rock	Shield	Hiding Place

You come to have confidence in God as you find new aspects of His nature through the events of your life. El Shaddai is my All-Sufficient One, Jehovah-rapha is the Lord who Heals, Jehovah-raah is the Lord my Shepherd.

None of you will receive His revelation in exactly the same way or the same order or the same intensity. But you will know that you know Him.

You can thank the Father for revealing Himself to you uniquely, personally, and through all of the experiences of life. Look expectantly for new evidences of Who He is.

Joyfully, Joyce

Worship God

6

Have you read Psalm 148 lately? There is a whole lot of praise going on. How excited do you get with Psalm 149: 1-3. Jump on over to Psalm 150! Think of the joy and privilege of praising God! This is quite a gathering: singing, dancing, instruments, shouts of joy, young and old, men and women, lifting up the name of the Lord! It is a real Praise Fest, and God is the focus. Who is this God that brings on our highest praise? Psalm 25:10 "Who is this King of glory The Lord of Hosts, He is the King of glory." Can you imagine joining in with the mighty chorus, hands raised in praise to God. Halleujah! Halleujah! Amen.

Use the Psalms to praise Him. Here are some ways to worship God:

sing, bless – Psalm 96:2   lift up hands – Psalm 63:4

Give thanks – Psalm 106:47   be glad, sing, rejoice Psalm 5:11

praise – Psalm 52:9   boast, praise – Psalm 44:8

trust, seek – Psalm 9:10   glory – Psalm 106:47

bow down, sing praise – Psalm 66:4   acclaim – Psalm 89:15.

Give yourself time this week to personally praise God, worship Him, adore Him, bless Him. Use the names of God you have experienced to praise Him. Be creative with your praise. Psalm 22:3 states that God is enthroned in the praises of His people. You are entering into His very presence with your praise.

Psalm 100:4
Enter into His gates with thanksgiving
And into His courts with praise.

Psalm 103:1
Bless the Lord, O my soul
And all that is within me bless His holy Name!

I Chronicles 29:11
Yours, O Lord, is the greatness
The power and the glory,
The victory and the majesty;
For all that is in heaven and in earth is Yours;

Yours is the kingdom, O Lord,
And you are exalted as head over all.

Enjoy His presence. Experience God!

Joyfully, Joyce

Loving God

7

What is the greatest commandment?

> You shall love the Lord your God
> With all your heart
> With all your soul
> With all your strength
> And with all your mind. Luke 10:27

That sounds wonderful, especially when you already know God loves you, that He is trustworthy, and that He wants your relationship to grow.

This commandment doesn't sound like it is asking for a begrudging, half-hearted attempt at love. In fact, Hannah Whitall Smith calls it utter abandonment to God, which is quite a startling word picture.

> How is this love going to be measured?
> Whoever has my commands and obeys them,
> he is the one who loves me.
> he who loves me will be loved by my Father,
> And I too will love him
> And show myself to him. John 14:21

You have to have actions to follow your words! And what are the benefits? You will be loved by the Father, loved by the Son, and Jesus will show Himself to you.

> How is God defined?
> God is love. I John 4:16

So, when you abandon yourself to God, you experience His very nature and presence: *LOVE!*"

God's love for you means His total acceptance of you. When you love God, you give Him your total acceptance as well.

- Accept His direction as best for you
- Accept His power to accomplish His will in you

- Accept His commandments as perfect guidelines for you

God is good!

Joyfully, Joyce

Learning God's Plan

8

God has a unique way of working in this world. Amazingly enough He has His own plan. So often we think it is necessary to come up with our plan and then ask God to bless our brilliant idea! There is a better way:

> Noah – God called him and gave him an exact building plan for the Ark

> Abraham – He was called out of his comfort zone to join the plan of God

> Moses - He found out there were much better results when he followed the plan of God.

It was up to each of these normal, ordinary people to hear, recognize, and decide to follow the call that God gave.

Praise God, you are not expected to come up with a plan and ask God to approve. That gets poor results and can get you in a peck of trouble. Sarah tried to hurry up the plan by sending her handmaid in to Abraham. The results were a disaster.

What about your area of ministry? Are you spending time in prayer asking God to show you where He is already working? God is preparing hearts right now to seek Him and desire to hear His message of love. Will you be available to share it? Sometimes you are called to be still, to be quiet before God, to look and listen. Then you can reach out to those He has already touched, when they ask you.

Perhaps it is a chance meeting (or is it a Divine Appointment?) of someone at the Mall, or a new friend where you are working. The key will be that they _want_ to know, they have already been seeking, already been praying to know about the way to God.

Praise God when you are just the available servant ready to show the way to the King of Kings. Henry Blackaby's special statement in <u>Experiencing God</u> is:

Look to see where God is working and join Him!

Joyfully, Joyce

Learning Through The Word

9

God speaks to you personally through His Word. Be alert to listen for what He has to say to you. This is part of an intimate love relationship with God. As you read the Word daily, perhaps a special phrase or line will impress you or stick in your mind. <u>Expect</u> God to speak to you.

Today I was reading Numbers 23:12. God impressed me with the words:

Must I not take heed to speak what the Lord has put in my mouth?

This came as I struggled to speak to a close friend about what God calls sin. As I meditate on this statement, I sense God telling me to speak His Word boldly, lovingly, directly, sincerely.

As you read the Word, realize that the Spirit of God is revealing spiritual truth to you. He is your private tutor to reveal Truth to you. God, through the Holy Spirit, your helper, your comforter, is teaching you personally-revealed truths from His Word, the Bible.

John 16:13 But when He, the Spirit of Truth has come, He will guide you into all truth.

I Corinthians 2:12 Now we have received not the spirit of the world but the Spirit who is from God, that we might know the things that have been freely given us by God.

Psalm 119 is an entire chapter (176 verses) honoring God's Word. It is called His statutes, precepts, laws, commandments, judgments, Word, testimonies.

Psalm 119:12 Blessed are you O Lord
Teach me your statutes
(This is repeated 9 times in this Psalm)

Psalm 119:18   Open my eyes that I may behold
Wondrous things from your law.

Allow Him to teach you. Listen for His message to you today. Write down what He impresses you to remember. Meditate on it, pray through it, receive His lesson. Be prepared. Be expecting it.

Joyfully, Joyce

How God Answers Prayer

10

Ask and you shall receive that your joy may be full. John 16:24

He can ...open the windows of heaven and pour out such blessing there will not be room enough to receive it. Malachi 3:10

He is...able to do exceedingly abundantly above all that we ask or think. Ephesians 3:20

Did you ever think that your prayers to God are too small? When you pray, give God permission to give you <u>more</u> than you ask. In fact, you should be willing to cancel your request in order to receive God's greater blessing. Often your vision limits your expectations of God. The prayer of Jabez in

I Chronicles 4:10 is powerful. It opens the door to expect more.

> And Jabez called on the God of Israel saying, Oh, that You would bless me indeed, and enlarge my territory, that Your hand would be with me, and that You would keep me from evil, that I may not cause pain! So God granted him what he requested.

> Eye has not seen nor ear heard the things God has prepared for them that love Him. I Corinthians 2:9

Father, help me to trust you so much that even when I pray, I allow you to increase the blessing You desire to give. In Jesus' name, Amen.

Life is and adventure.

Expect God's blessing.

Expect bigger things than you ask for.

Enjoy the ride!

Joyfully, Joyce

Trust Through
The Tough Times

||

Job was tested by Satan with God's permission. Job lost family and possessions. He endured painful sores on his body, yet his faith remained.

> The Lord gives and the Lord takes away,
> Blessed be the name of the Lord. Job 1:21

> I know that my Redeemer lives
> And that He shall stand at last on the earth…
> How my heart yearns within me! Job 19:25-27

David spoke of his faith in God through the tough times:

> Yea though I walk through the valley of the shadow of death I will fear no evil for You are with me. Psalm 23:4

God has promised to go through the valley with you. Confusion comes when you try to understand your situation in the middle of the tough times. It is like looking in a distorted mirror. Everything seems strange and out of focus. It may not make sense to you. Instead, look to the Word for help, understanding and comfort.

The most important fact in difficult times is to know that <u>God knows</u> where you are. And He is right there with you.

> If I take the wings of the morning and dwell in the uttermost parts of the sea Your Hand shall lead me and Your Right Hand shall hold me. Psalm 139:9

When times are tough, focus on the Word. Let God show you TRUTH to cling to. Ask God to show you His perspective on your circumstances and situation. Let the Holy Spirit use the Word to reveal God's view.

Pray this way: Father, I desire to know You in the easy times and the difficult times. Thank you for never leaving me or forsaking me. Thank you for being my Guide. Your perspective upon the mountain is so much greater than mine in the valley. In Jesus' name, Amen

Joyfully, Joyce

Faith In Action

12

When God calls you to join Him, He is likely to show you God-sized projects. This brings you to a point of decision. You must decide how big your God is. Are you willing to take a giant step of faith? Will you trust that God who called you will accomplish His work? It will be obvious that the job cannot succeed without God's divine intervention.

Joshua had a decision to make when God gave him instructions to conquer Jericho. He was to simply march around the city every day for seven days. Joshua knew that for success the result would have to be God's work. Joshua 6

Gideon's army was finally reduced to 300 men –

to fight an army of hundreds of thousands. Gideon had to decide if he would follow God's call and leave the results to God. The battle cry was, "The sword of the Lord and of Gideon." Judges 7

Now faith is the substance of things hoped for, the evidence of things not seen.
Hebrews 11:1

True faith is revealed by our actions.

Hear God.

Take the step.

Expect God-size results.

It's not about you. It's all about Him.

Father, help us to listen for your voice, hear your clear instruction, and move forward. Your work… Your Victory… Your Praise!!!

Joyfully, Joyce

Being Part Of The Body of Christ

13

As a child, you learned to draw people: legs, arms, torso, head. Later you added hands, feet, eyes, nose, mouth. All of these components, and more, makes a whole person.

> Feet are necessary
> Hands are important
> Eyes are vital
> Ears are needed
> All organs must work together

The Bible tells us we are parts together of Christ's body, the church. Every part has a function to make the body complete. Every part is valuable and works to allow the whole body to fulfill its purpose.

You are an important part of the body of Christ: His church! You can look to see what God is doing in your church and choose to join Him in His work. You need to ask God's direction in serving. Each church experience is a wonderful opportunity to join the loving, moving, functioning body of Christ.

Bloom where you are planted! Rejoice in the church where God leads you. Serve Him joyfully. Hear His voice. Be willing to say, "Whatever You ask, Lord, I will do it."

Joyfully, Joyce

Taking A Step Of Faith

14

Have you ever felt like you are way over your head in the work God has called you to do? Good! You are in good company. It is ok to feel over-whelmed. God calls you not for your great ability, but for your availability in faith.

> God spoke to David and David spoke his faith:
> The battle is the Lord's. I Samuel 17:47
> The battle plan included a few stones and a slingshot!

> God talked to Moses and Moses spoke his faith to the people:
> Stand still and see the salvation of the Lord. Exodus 14:13

The waters of the Red Sea conquered the Egyptian army. God gave the victory. God got the glory.

Did Peter expect 3,000 people to accept his message and become followers of Jesus on the Day of Pentecost? (See Acts 2) No, he simply gave the message that God gave him. God brought the increase. God got the glory.

Each time God does a great work through your weakness, God gets the glory!

Allow yourself to serve a God who causes you to do work so big that only He can account for the results. When you do, God gets the credit.

It takes a step of faith to say Yes, Lord, to a God-size challenge.

- Gideon felt inadequate. "Why me," he said in Judges 6.
- Moses was afraid when God first spoke to him. "Choose someone else," he said, Exodus 4.

Faith is the key to allowing God to accomplish

great things through you. Be prepared to say with Isaiah:

Here am I, Lord, send me. Isaiah 6:8

And leave the results to Him.
And let Him get the glory.

Joyfully, Joyce

Action!

15

Have you heard the statement: Actions speak louder than words!

Your actions reveal what you really believe. Do you believe God has spoken to you? Are you challenged to trust Him? Do you believe God desires to accomplish His will through you?

Faith builds up in you. It leads you to conviction. It leads you to a decision.

> Noah built an ark. (Genesis 6:22)
> Abraham left his homeland. (Genesis 12:4)
> Peter got out of the boat. (Matthew 14:29)

The woman touched the hem of Jesus' garment. (Mathew 9:21)

David stood up to Goliath (I Samuel 17:45-50)

Moses raised his staff at the Red Sea (Exodus 14:21)

These heroes all had faith in God. Their actions demonstrated what they believed.

Hebrews 11 gives us a hall of heroes.

They all made a decision to act on their faith. Their action was a visible demonstration of their faith in the God Who spoke to them.

I have decided to follow Jesus

Will you go with me?

Joyfully, Joyce

Follow Me

16

Have you noticed that those who accept God's call are willing to change? It takes more than a decision to follow, it also requires action.

> Peter and Andrew left their nets. Matthew 4:20
> Matthew left his profitable tax job. Matthew 9:9
> Zacchaeus changed his business plan. Luke 19:8

> But unfortunately the rich young ruler refused to take action. Luke 18:23

What was the difference between the men of faith and the rich young ruler? It was the willingness to change and take action. The spiritual decision (faith) must be accompanied by the physical action (change).

For whoever desires to save his life will lose it, but whoever loses his life for my sake will save it. Luke 9:24

You must be willing to come to Jesus with open hands – holding out your hopes, desires, plans, goals and possessions. Give God all that you treasure, and in return He will give you His best.

Anyone who does not give up everything he has cannot be my disciples. Luke 14:33

There is a simple, single word you can speak in prayer, it is

WHATEVER, LORD

Let all your pride, goals and ambitions be held in open hands to God. And then you tell Him: whatever. The returns far exceed what you bring. God is delighted to give back more, abundantly more, than what you offer. He is lavish in His giving!

Ephesians 3:17, 18 explains how God opens your eyes,

that Christ may dwell in your hearts through faith; that you, being rooted and grounded in love, may be able to comprehend with all the saints what is the width and length and depth, and height – to know the love of Christ which passes knowledge, that you may be filled with all the fullness of God.

Joyfully, Joyce

Interruptions From God

17

God may sometimes take the opportunity to interrupt you right in the middle of your plans and programs. It is ok. In fact, it is necessary at those times to adjust your plans to join God in what He is doing. Be sensitive to what the Holy Spirit is telling you.

God may have a greater assignment for you than you think you can handle. Don't be surprised. God's assignments are often super-sized. Just like a fast food meal! Remember, if God calls you to a task, He is also there to help you accomplish the work to be done. Working with God in this way gives Him the glory for the success. The Holy Spirit is your Guide, your Counselor, and your Teacher. Be willing to meet God on His schedule.

Doing the extraordinary (a God-sized assignment) may mean leaving the ordinary (what you can handle alone) and letting God do a greater work in and through you.

> Are some people asking about your faith? Set aside your plans and share with them.

> Do some acquaintances want to start a Bible Study? Be available to start one.

> Has someone asked to be Discipled? Now is the time to do it.

Proverbs 3:5,6
> Trust in the Lord with all your heart
> And lean not on your own understanding
> In all your ways acknowledge Him
> And He shall direct your paths.

Will you pray this way: Lord, please interrupt my plans any time you have a greater assignment for me.

Joyfully, Joyce

Connected To The Vine

18

When and where God leads you, He will provide for you. He will not simply give you a plan or a method and expect you to do it on your own. Your living, loving Heavenly Father is constantly at work in you. To fulfill God's plan means you must stay connected to Him in close relationship.

John 15:5 I am the vine you are the branches.
  If a man remains in me and I in him,
  he will bear much fruit;
  apart from me you can do nothing.

Staying connected is the key. The vine provides the nourishment, the strength, the energy to allow the branches to grow strong. It is the LIFE. It is only that connection which can produce fruit.

Only God knows His purposes and only God can accomplish them. The plans and their results are much bigger than you and I can see. Allow God's view to take over.

I Corinthians 2:9,10
> Eye has not seen nor ear heard
> Nor has entered into the heart of man
> The things which God has purposed
> For those who love Him.

But God has revealed them to us through His Spirit

This means you must have total dependence on God. Nothing can take the place of your relationship with Him. He reveals His plan to us one day at a time.

Stay connected.

Allow for daily quiet time with Him.

Enjoy His presence throughout each day.

Be filled with the Spirit.

Joyfully, Joyce

Spiritual Gifts

19

At birthdays children are always so excited about gifts. There is such joy in receiving and opening the special packages from loved ones. God also loves to gives special gifts to His children.

Henry Blackaby defines spiritual gifts in his book Experiencing God,

> A supernatural empowering to accomplish the assignment God gives you.

In I Corinthians 12:4-11, where it speaks about spiritual gifts, the emphasis is on the Spirit; the Lord; God: Who is assigning and distributing gifts as He chooses. In Ephesians 4:11-13 it states that He gave spiritual assignments for equipping and edifying the body...

> till we all come to the unity of the faith, and of the knowledge of the Son of God, to a perfect man, to the measure of the stature of the fullness of Christ.

The emphasis is not on what spiritual gift you have, but on your relationship with God. It is the Holy Spirit who is working in and through you. God chooses, God designs, God calls, God equips. It is not difficult to determine Who is in charge.

Your focus is on a close relationship with the Father so you are equipped to serve whenever and wherever He calls you. Just as the gifts you receive at Christmas relate to the special relationship you have with your loved ones, so your Father chooses what is best for you.

Assignments will come and divine appointments will occur throughout your life, but your relationship with the Father lasts forever.

From the song, "In the Garden,"

And He walks with me and He talks with
me
And He tells me I am His own
And the joy we share as we tarry there
None other has ever known.

Joyfully, Joyce

The Church Is Alive

20

Praise God for the church in every location. God intends for you to be connected. He wants you to work through the church. He wants you to be to be under the umbrella of protection of the church. Where you are living and serving is the place God has chosen. You add an important dimension to your local body of believers.

The church **is** the <u>Body</u>, Christ is the Head. We need to cherish and honor the leaders and believers as much as Christ does.

> Ephesians 5:25, 26 …Christ also loved the church and gave Himself for her, that He might sanctify and cleanse her with the wash-

ing of water by the word, that He might present her to Himself a glorious church, not having spot or wrinkle or any such thing, but that she should be holy and without blemish.

Praise God for the church that sends you out and supports you in your efforts. They are your prayer warriors. They are to be honored. And praise God for the fellowship of believers where He places you to serve. Whether the assignment is short or long, this is your place to serve as a member. Use your gifts to nourish, strengthen, and cherish. To honor and respect the church is to honor Christ.

Like any individual, each church will have strengths and weaknesses. It will have its own character. But your purpose in being there is to edify, to encourage focus on God, to serve gladly, joyfully and sacrificially.

There were letters to churches in Corinth, Galatia, Ephesus, Colossai, Philippi, Thessalonica, and Rome. All these churches were different, but all epitomized Christ's body in that location.

Here are church instructions in Colossians 3:12-16,

> Therefore, as the elect of God, holy and beloved, put on tender mercies, kindness, humility, meekness, longsuffering, bearing with one another. If anyone has a complaint against another, even as Christ forgave you, so you also must do. But above all these things put on love which is the bond of perfection. And let the peace of God rule in your hearts, to which also you were called in one body; and be thankful.

You see, it's not about me, it's all loving one another and about honoring God.

Joyfully, Joyce

The Body Of Believers

21

The church is a body of believers that God has brought together in one location. He adds members to complement one another in service. God is actively involved, because the Holy Spirit Who IS the Gift, is there to assign gifts as needed for the body of believers.

Each member has value and purpose. God prepares and builds up members to fulfill His assignment for that church at that time and place!

How exciting to see God add members especially designed to fulfill ministry. Being a part of God's church is never dull!

As Henry Blackaby encourages,

> Look to see where God is working and join Him.

Joyfully, Joyce

Prepared For Service

22

Romans 12:1,2 suggests that you can have an intimate, ongoing, consistent love relationship with God. It is definitely worth pursuing.

> Present your body a living sacrifice, holy, acceptable to God which is your reasonable service.

> Be transformed by the renewing of your mind, that you may prove what God's good and acceptable will is for you.

Learning God's will for you is found in the Word. God speaks to you through the Word. Jesus IS the Word. Your connection to the Word will give you guidance, direction, focus, and peace of mind. You need to seek God's leading on a daily basis. This is your Book of Instructions, your personal Atlas and road map!

Philippians 4:8 encourages you to meditate on these things:

> Whatever things are noble, whatever things are just,
> whatever things are pure, whatever things are lovely,
> whatever things are of good report, if there is any
> virtue and anything praiseworthy.

As you read God's love letter to you, there will be clear focus on what God asks of you.

> Psalm 119:11 Your Word I have hid in my heart that I might not sin against You.

> Joshua 1:8 This Book of the Law shall not depart from your mouth, but you shall meditate in it day and night, that you may observe to do according to all that is written in it.

Put into practice what you learn there. That is God's will for you.

Joyfully, Joyce

Purpose

23

When you consider your life and want to know your purpose, you need to look to God. Ask Him. He is the Creator. Only He can show you the reason He made you.

Colossians 1:16b states: All thing were made through Him and for Him.

Finding the answer to these basic questions, will transform your life:

Who am I?

What am I here for?

Before you were born, God knew all about you.

Psalm 139: 14,16
I will praise You for I am fearfully and won-
derfully made.
Marvelous are Your works and that my soul
knows very well.
Your eyes saw my substance being yet
unformed,
And in Your book they all were written
The days fashioned for me, when as yet there
were none of them.

God has a plan for your life: Jeremiah 29:11,
12:

For I know the plans that I have for you, says
the Lord,
Plans for good and not for evil, to give you a
future and a hope.

God participated in your creation. He values
you. You are loved. Your purpose Is wrapped up in
why God made you.

Joyfully, Joyce

God's Design

24

Psalm 139:17 states:

> How precious also are Your thoughts to me,
>   O God,
> How great is the sum of them!
> If I should count them, they would be
> more in number than the sand!
> When I awake, I am still with You.

God's plan and His purpose are wrapped up in the fact that that He loves <u>you!</u> He is thinking about you all the time. Psalm 139:15-16 beautifully describes God's involvement in your beginnings even before birth.

> My frame was not hidden from You,
> When I was made in secret,

And skillfully wrought in the
Lowest parts of the earth.
Your eyes saw my substance,
being yet unformed,
And in Your book they all were written,
The days fashioned for me,
When as yet there were none of them.

Each aspect of who you are, the things you like and the things you dislike about yourself are all part of God's design. You are this person, in this generation, from this family, raised in this country, with this personality and skin color, all a part of God's excellent design.

I will praise You, for I am fearfully and
wonderfully made.
Marvelous are Your works,
And that my soul knows very well. Psalm
139: 14

Rejoice in the thought that you are exactly the person God planned you to be. Because of that, He has arranged for you to serve and minister in this certain place at this particular time.

Praise Him for loving you so much.

Joyfully, Joyce

Past To Present

25

All of your past has shaped you into the person you are today. God uses who we are, and all of those past experiences, the good, the bad and the ugly, to define the ministry He has for us. Begin to thank God for the miracle of transforming the negatives - disappointments, hurts, fears, anger - into positives in your life. You are, by God's grace, His chosen beloved child. You have been given a holy calling by the Father for ministry.

You may have let your past hold you back from experiencing the presence of God, but God wants to set you free. Freedom comes when you release the past by thanking God for it. Let it go. Praise Him.

Romans 8:2 states:

> For the law of the Spirit of life in Christ Jesus
> Made me free from the law of sin and death.

My friend, when God sets you free, you are free indeed!

> Pray this prayer: Lord, I release my past. I know that you are able to make all things work together for good.
> In You I find my purpose, my fulfillment, my joy. Thank you for the freedom that You give.

Gloria Gather wrote:

> Something beautiful, something good
> All my confusion He understood
> All I had to offer Him was brokenness and strife
> But He made something beautiful
> Of my life

Today is a new day that God has packaged and designed for you. Give yourself permission to receive it and serve Him gladly.

Finally let go of the past. Reach out to the joy of being in the presence of the Father.

Philippians 3:13

> Forgetting those things which are behind and reaching forward to those things which are ahead, I press toward the goal of the prize of the upward call of God in Christ Jesus.

Joyfully, Joyce

Our Olympics

26

John 14:2 states: In my Father's house are many mansions…

While the world warns, This is the beginning of the end! God tells us, the end is just the beginning! We have eternity to look forward to. Choices we make now count for eternity.

Rick Warren states in his book, <u>The Purpose Driven Life</u>,

The deeds of this life are the destiny of the next.

Make what you do today <u>count</u> for eternity.

Lighten your load and let go of the unimportant things that hold you back. Let go of the things that hold you down. Focus on the goal. Seek first the kingdom of God.

> Hebrews 12:1, 2 puts it so well:
> Therefore, we also, since we are surrounded
> by so great a cloud of witnesses (cheering!)
> let us lay aside every weight,
> and the sin which so easily ensnares us,
> and let us run with endurance the race that is
> set before us,
> looking unto Jesus the author and finisher of
> our faith...

Focus on Jesus
Follow His example
Find your purpose.

The Olympics of your life is now and it counts for Eternity.

Joyfully, Joyce

Times Of Testing

27

How do you look at times of testing? Is there fear, dread, sadness? It is much like going to the dentist. You know there will be pain, it will be difficult, but you have to endure it in order to get the end result.

Paul shares an important insight in Romans 5:3
> And not only that, but we also glory in tribulations, knowing that tribulation produces perseverance; and perseverance character; and character, hope.

Paul looked forward to the end result, and he saw character-building attributes coming from tribulation. Paul also knew you would not have to do it alone. That is why you can glory in tribulations.

When you look at God's over-all plan and see His purpose and protection in all things, then tribulations will not overwhelm you.

James had a similar view in James 1:2

> My brethren, count it all joy when you fall into various trials, knowing that the testing of your faith produces patience. But let patience have its perfect work, that you may be perfect and complete, lacking nothing.

Again the conclusion is that testing has a purpose. God is using each challenge in your life to mold and shape you into the likeness of Jesus.

I Peter 1:5, 6 states that you are:

> <u>kept by the power of God</u> through faith for salvation, ready to be revealed in the last time. In this you greatly rejoice, though now for a little while, if need be, you have been grieved by various trials, that the genuineness of your faith…may be found to praise, honor, and glory at the revelation of Jesus Christ.

How you handle the trials, tests, and tribulations of life, depends on how you view your Father.

When a typhoon strikes, people find a safe place, protected from the storm. You also have a safe place of protection.

> Psalm 91 begins: He who dwells in the secret place of the Most High, shall abide under the shadow of the Almighty.

Turn to Him. Place your trust in Him.

Joyfully, Joyce

Ambassadors

28

Ambassadors are necessarily representatives of their nation. It is an assignment and a privilege. They do not have an agenda of their own, but carry out the wishes of their leader. Wherever you go, whatever you do, you are God's Ambassador. You are representing your homeland, Heaven. You represent your King, Jesus, Ruler of heaven and earth.

Proverbs 13:17: A faithful ambassador brings health.

Here on earth you are called foreigner, stranger, pilgrim, alien, sojourner. That is ok, because your citizenship is in heaven. Peter urges that your conduct be honorable because you are an ambassador. I Peter

2:11, 12. Your stay on earth is short before you are recalled to your heavenly mansion where you will live forever with your Father.

Look beyond earthly possessions and continue on your journey joyfully because you anticipate your true homeland, Heaven. Many have arrived there already, and they are now a cloud of witnesses on your behalf. They also were once strangers and pilgrims, but they were seeking a city not built with hands, Hebrews 11. They are the ones cheering you on.

Pray for all of God's ambassadors that they may speak boldly, and represent Him well.

Joyfully, Joyce

The Glory Of God

29

Much of the Bible speaks about the glory of God. Psalm 19:1: The heavens declare the glory of God, and the firmament shows His handiwork.

You can see the handiwork of God in majestic mountains, rolling waves of the ocean, colorful birds and fish and flowers, the intricate detail of each part of His creation, as well as the vastness of the universe. These all speak of the glory of God.

David devotes many Psalms to extolling the glory of God: praising Him, thanking Him, honoring Him, rejoicing in what He created.

When the Word became flesh, we...

Beheld His <u>glory</u>, glory as of the only begotten of the Father, full of grace and truth.
John 1:14.

O Lord our Lord, how excellent is Your name
in all the earth

Who have set your <u>glory</u> above the heavens.
Psalm 8:1

To God alone wise, be <u>glory</u> through Jesus
Christ forever. Amen

Romans 16:27

Sing to Him, sing psalms to Him, talk of all
His wondrous works. <u>Glory</u> in His holy
name. I Chronicles 16:9,10

But he who glories, let him <u>glory</u> in the Lord.
II Corinthians 10:17

…that in all things God may be <u>glorified</u>
through Jesus Christ,

To whom belong the <u>glory</u> and the domin-
ion forever and ever. Amen

I Peter 4:11

I pray that you can see you are to focus on the
glory of God. Your purpose is to declare the glory of
God. You are to acknowledge His glory. You are to
honor, announce, praise, reflect – on the glory of God.
Your purpose is to bring glory to God by your life.

Jesus said: I have glorified You on the earth. I

have finished the work which You have given Me to do. John 17:4

Just like Jesus, you fulfill your purpose when you give glory to the Lord of Lords.

Joyfully, Joyce

God's Special Love

30

From the time you were conceived, God has loved you and taken pleasure in you. He formed your inmost parts. He covered you in your mother's womb. He sees you as a precious and beloved person. His love for you is unconditional. Psalm 139:13-18

> Before I formed you in the womb I knew you. Jeremiah 1:5
>
> I have loved you with an everlasting love. Jeremiah 31:3
>
> Many O Lord are Your wonderful works which You have done.
> And Your thoughts toward us cannot be recounted.

They are more than can be numbered. Psalm
40:5

God thinks you are special, important and valued. You need to look at yourself in the same way as God sees you.

If God is for us, who can be against us! Romans 8:31

Because God really, really loves you, He has a provided a way for you to respond to Him. That response to God is called worship. Your worship brings pleasure to God because you are responding to His love. True worship involves passion and commitment. Once you see God loves you so much and freely gives you all things, responding to Him is natural. Worship focuses on God.

God so loved <u>you</u> that He gave His only begotten Son. You are worth it!

See yourself as God sees you: beloved, precious, valued. Respond to Him in worship.

Joyfully, Joyce

Just Like Noah

31

Would you be willing, like Noah, to live your life to be pleasing to God? That is really what God wants. Praising God brings Him pleasure and it brings us joy also.

> We sing the song, Thou Art Worthy. ...for You have created all things. And for <u>Your</u> pleasure they are created Thou art worthy, O Lord.

Noah found <u>grace</u> in the eyes of the Lord, Genesis 6:8. Can you please God like Noah? Noah accepted a close, love relationship with God. The Bible states that Enoch and Noah walked with God. Genesis 5:24 and 6:9. Loving God with heart, soul, mind and strength is sure to please Him. It is <u>responding</u> to His love.

Will you <u>trust</u> God like Noah? Trust is a way to please God.

Hebrews 11:6 states: Without faith it is impossible to please God.

Trust means expecting God will lead you perfectly in all your ways. Trust is taking God at His Word. We sing the song, Trust and Obey for there is no other way to be happy in Jesus but to trust and obey.

Will you <u>obey</u> God just like Noah? God desires glad obedience, joyful obedience, enthusiastic obedience, ready obedience. Move forward with what you are called to do.

Will you <u>praise</u> God when He brings you through a difficult time? Noah did that, too. His first act after leaving the ark was to praise and honor God.

> Psalm 103:1 states: Bless the Lord O my soul
> And all that is within me bless His holy name!

Finally, will you <u>use your gifts</u> and talents as a way to honor and please God? Noah and sons got right to work when they landed. God gives you special skills, so use them to glorify Him. Whatever you do, do all to the glory of God.

Rise, Shine, Give God the Glory!

Joyfully, Joyce

Taking a Risk

32

Are you willing to take a mighty Big Risk? Romans 12:1 starts out as a challenge, a call to lay your life on the line with God:

> I beseech you brethren by the mercies of God to present your bodies a living sacrifice, holy, acceptable unto God which is your reasonable service, Verse 2 concludes …that you may prove what is that good and acceptable and perfect will of God.

You are called to make a <u>decision</u>: choose to surrender – become a bondservant, a slave to righteousness, a living sacrifice.

This leads to <u>action</u>: sacrifice. You are called to allow God to use every circumstance for His Glory. This is where you have the biggest challenge, the biggest risk. Often you may pray to your Father and ask him to correct a situation. You may ask Him to change the circumstances. You ask for deliverance. You want relief. You want to see the problem fixed! But are you willing to take the Big Risk. Can you say: Lord, please <u>do not</u> answer my prayer if You determine that this difficult situation will bring glory to you! Lord, not my will, but Yours be done.

Do you trust Him that much? The result is significant <u>service</u>. God honors your trust and you are able to serve Him fully with God-anointed results. You will then be a willing, living sacrifice to God, accepting Him, trusting Him in a new spiritual dimension. You will be walking with Him in unity, allowing His mighty power to be evident each step of the way.

DECISION.....ACTION.....SERVICE

Joyfully, Joyce

Friendship With God

33

How amazing it is to think of being able to have a friendship with God. Moses and the Lord spoke as friends in the tabernacle. Exodus 33:11. How awesome that must have been. Abraham is referred to as God's friend forever. Isaiah 41:8. What a privilege.

Yet, God offers to each one of us the privilege of His friendship. God asks for your friendship. God encourages your friendship. God desires your friendship.

<u>Best friends share secrets:</u> In John 15:15 Jesus says that all things that He heard from the Father he has made known to us. I Corinthians 2:10 tells us that God has revealed the deep things of God to us through the Spirit.

<u>Best friends talk a lot.</u> Reading God's word allows you to hear from God and know His will. Sharing with Him your daily, intimate thoughts gives you that close relationship between friends. Talking to God can be an ongoing conversation with Him throughout your daily activities. I Thessalonians 5:17 encourages you to pray without ceasing.

<u>Best friends share good times and bad.</u> Matthew 11:28 states: Come to Me, all you who labor and are heavy laden, and I will give you rest. Hebrews 13:5 tells you: He will never leave you or forsake you. I Peter 5:7 says, Casting all your care upon Him for He cares for you.

<u>Best friends look out for one another and put each other first.</u> John 15:13 tells you: Greater love has no man than this, than to lay down one's life for his friends. Matthew 5:33 says to Seek first the kingdom of God and His righteousness.

<u>Best friends are loyal.</u> John 15:14 states, You are my friends if you do whatever I command you. Proverbs 18:24 states that there is a Friend who sticks closer than a brother!

<u>Best friends love to be together.</u> Adam walked in the garden with God. Moses spoke to Him in the tabernacle and on the mountain. David spent hours singing to God.

Have you accepted the offer to be Best Friends with God?

Joyfully, Joyce

Becoming a Close Friend of God

34

God honors honesty. When you come to Him, it is acceptable to tell God exactly how you feel. Too often it is easier to mask your feelings, or think that it is inappropriate to express your thoughts.

God is not hurt, surprised, horrified or angered if you talk to Him honestly.

Are you afraid, worried, hurt, mad, disappointed, frustrated, angry? It is ok to say so. You are in good company. Read the Psalms and see how David spoke to God. David and God were on a very personal level of friendship.

Only when you speak up, express your feelings,

admit what it is that bothers you, are you able to be free in your relationship with God. This is the point where you trust God enough to tell Him your innermost feelings.

This brings you to a new level of relationship. Only then can God help you work out His purpose in your life.

> Romans 8:28 states, And we know that all things work together for good to those that love God, to those who are called according to His purpose.

When God knows you trust Him enough to express your true feelings, he will lead you to a closer, fuller, intimate relationship with Him than you have had before. Out of this comes joy, praise, peace and comfort.

Confession is a choice. It is the right choice. Desiring to have friendship with God is the best choice.

Joyfully, Joyce

Offering a
Sacrifice to God

35

In the Old Testament times, giving a sacrifice was a common way of worship. The sacrifice spoke of atonement for sin. Either a lamb or a dove was brought by individuals and given to the priest to be used for sacrifice. The sacrifice was the giving of something of value. There was meaning to the donor because it was the very best that he could afford. It was presented to God as a payment for sin.

When Christ came, he became the sacrificial Lamb, whose blood was shed for the sins of the world.

Psalm 51:16, 17 shows that David understands the heart of God:

> For You do not desire sacrifice, or else I
>   would give it.
> You do not delight in burnt offering.
> The sacrifices of God are a broken spirit,
> A broken and a contrite heart –
> These, O God, You will not despise

Sacrifice is a matter of the heart. It is taking something that you value, something that you would keep for yourself, but instead you willingly hand it to God.

> Psalm 54:6 I will freely sacrifice to You,
> I will praise Your name O Lord.

> Psalm 141:2 Let my prayer be set before You
>   as incense
> The lifting up of my hands as the evening
>   sacrifice.

> Hebrews 13:16 But do not forget to do good
>   and share
> For with such sacrifices God is well pleased.

Finally, the ultimate gift you can give to God is to lift yourself to Him:

> Romans 12:1 I beseech you therefore, brethren, that you present

Your bodies a living sacrifice, holy, acceptable
    unto God
Which is your reasonable service.

Sacrifice your time, your talents, your praise,
your contrite heart, to your God Who loved you
enough to sacrifice His only begotten Son.

Joyfully, Joyce

Trusting Jesus In The Darkness

36

Jesus is the same yesterday, today, and forever. He never changes.

Jesus is the Anchor. He is the Firm Foundation, the Solid Rock. He is the Chief Cornerstone, the Living Stone, my Rock, my Fortress, My Deliverer, my Shield, my Strength, and my Salvation. He is all of these things: yesterday, today and forever. (Psalm 18:1-3, Hebrews 13:8)

When you do not feel God near, when feelings let you down, cling To Who Jesus is. Hold to the Anchor in the storms of life, stand on the Solid Rock, be protected by your Fortress, your Shield.

Only when you go through tough times, when God seems silent and you cannot feel Him, will you experience Him completely through faith.

You need to call out the Name of Jesus. You need to know the names of Jesus that identify Who He really is.

Psalm 46:1 states: God is our refuge and strength
A very present help in trouble.

Hebrews 11:1 Faith is the substance…
Faith is the evidence…

Hebrews 11:6 Without faith it is impossible to please God.

Trust Him in the darkness
Trust Him in the silence
Cling to the Word

Joyfully, Joyce

Your Family Heritage

37

What is your heritage? What are your family ties? Have there been famous people in your family history, great leaders or kings? Are you proud of your nationality? Many conventions each year celebrate national heritage: Italian, Dutch, Swedish, Irish and many more. All take great pride in family name, coat of arms, and achievement. Asians honor their ancestors in many ways.

Each new Christian is announced and welcomed into the Family of God. There is great rejoicing in Heaven when you accept the gift God gives.

John 1:12 says that when you receive Jesus, you are given the privilege of becoming children of God – part of God's family.

Your pride is being united with brothers and sisters in God's Family. We belong to each other, we have a single heritage. We care for one another, help one another, love one another.

Bill and Gloria Gaither wrote a song years ago:
I m so glad I'm a part of the family of God. I've been washed in the fountain, Cleansed by His blood, Joint Heirs with Jesus as we travel this sod, For I'm part of the family, the family of God.

You have the confirmation of the Holy Spirit telling you that you belong to God s family. Romans 8:16

Here is your heritage:
> You are a family member, an heir Galatians 4:7
>
> You have a heavenly citizenship Philippians 3:20
>
> You have God's riches Philippians 4:19
>
> You have a caring family who loves you fervently I Peter 4:8
>
> You have the Comforter living in you John 14:17
>
> You have treasures in heaven Matthew 6:20

You have a home prepared for you by Jesus
John 14:2

You have everlasting life John 3:16

Rejoice in your own special Family. Your Father adores you!

Joyfully, Joyce

Love One Another

38

John 13:34 states,

> A new commandment I give to you, that you love one another; as I have loved you, that you also love one another.

A command is not a choice. Therefore, for Christians, love is a decision but not a choice. God calls us to love our brothers and sisters. I Peter 4:8. We are family, we are one.

The Ten Commandments have one theme: LOVE: First, Love God, and Second Love others. Luke 10:27. This puts your life in perspective. Love in action will color and influence everything you do.

I Corinthians 13 describes love and its importance on actions. Any effort without love is empty, useless, futile, dead. Love gives life to your actions. Love makes your life meaningful – it expresses Who God is through you. God is Love!

Rick Warren states in his book, <u>The Purpose Driven Life,</u>

> You can give without loving, but you cannot love without giving.

We celebrate Jesus who is the epitome of God's love. Let love define your life. Let it be your <u>decision</u> to follow Jesus' example and His command.

May the love of God shine through every gift and action.

Joyfully, Joyce

A Member Of The Family of God

39

It is important to belong. Your sense of belonging gives you confidence, security, and peace. Just as growing up in a loving, functional family helps you mature, so being a member of a loving, functioning church helps you mature spiritually.

You need your family and your family is not complete without you. Thousands of families today have a son or daughter overseas in the war in Iraq. Those families long for that loved one to return home safely. Then the family is complete. So it is in the church.

God gives you the church, a local body of believers, where you can be a member. This gives you nurture, protection, love, service – all facets of the fellowship. Just as God gives you the Word – for doctrine, reproof, correction, instruction in righteousness, (II Timothy 3:16) so God gives you a church where you can be connected and grow in all of those areas. Let the church teach you, encourage you, love you, send you.

How you are able to serve in God's kingdom is determined by how you commit yourself first to your church. Rick Warren states in his book, <u>The Purpose Driven Life</u>,

> Following God includes <u>belonging</u>, not just believing.

Christ loved the church. He gave His life for the church, His Bride. The church is your spiritual family. Your spiritual gifts and abilities are given for you to serve your church family. This is your purpose, your spiritual service.

Love the church where God places you. Serve the church joyfully. Make the church your priority. Grow and bloom where God plants you. So pray, encourage, serve, teach, honor, submit, be devoted, be accountable – all of this is your responsibility and commitment to the church.

God bless you as you commit yourself to your church family, and just watch how God allows you to grow.

Joyfully, Joyce

Fellowship In The Family

40

Small group fellowship is an important part of your Christian life. Close fellowship with Christians gives you caring, commitment, prayer partners, discipleship and accountability. In much of the world, Christians meet regularly only in small house groups, a mirror of the original small groups of the first church. Being able to meet each week with a small group gives you a bonding and oneness.

The Bible says: That which we have seen and heard we declare to you that you also may have fellowship with us, and truly our fellowship is with the Father and with His Son Jesus Christ. I John 1:3

> And they continued steadfastly in the apostle's doctrine and fellowship, in the breaking of bread and prayers. Acts 2:46

In the early church there were groups that met daily to share together. Such meetings assure that no one is left alone. You are also inviting Jesus into your group.

> And Jesus said: where two or three of you are together because of Me, you can be sure that I'll be there. Matthew 18:20 (Message translation)

> confess your sins one to another, pray for one another that you may be healed. The effectual fervent prayer of a righteous man avails much. James 5:16

We need to be there for each other in the hard times. You need the correction and encouragement of your loving brothers and sisters. You need to have Christians near you who know your tests and trials and who will commit to pray for you without ceasing.

> I John 1:7 states: If we walk in the light as

He is in the light we have fellowship with one another.

How often we worship in a large church and enjoy the praise and message, but the heart aches to have issues healed through close fellowship of caring Christians. Being in the light is being a faithful, believing Christian, and having fellowship with other Christians. There in a small group you can be open and vulnerable, trusting them with your joys and sorrows and questions. There you will find love, comfort, blessing and growth. You may speak what is on your heart, and receive counsel and understanding.

Joyfully, Joyce

Friendship In The Family

41

The Bible encourages you to be committed to your brothers and sisters in Christ. Your fellowship group is your family. You are called to love each one fervently. You need to depend on each other for help, strength, encouragement, prayer, and guidance.

Ephesians 4:3 calls us to: Endeavor to keep the unity of the Spirit in the bond of peace.

You need to cling to those words. Put your brothers first. Be ready to reach out in prayer and love. You are a part of the lifeline for each one in your group. You also need to be willing to receive the same commitment from your fellowship group.

You are called on to speak the truth in love. (Ephesians 4:15)

You must earn the right to help those in your fellowship by having a loving, trusting relationship with the Lord and with your friend. Sin is like leaven. It does not just affect one person, but it touches the entire group. You need to care enough to share truth lovingly. You need to care enough to reach out.

> Galatians 6:1 Gently help one another... Bear one another's burdens, if someone falls into sin, forgivingly restore him.

> Romans 12:9-15 gives us the standard to follow:
> *Let love be without hypocrisy *Abhor evil
> *Cling to good *Be devoted to one another
> *Give preference *Be fervent in spirit
> *Serve the Lord *Rejoice in hope
> *Be patient in tribulation *Continuing in prayer
> *Rejoice with those who rejoice, weep with those who weep.

The *Message* translates Romans 15:1, 2 this way:

Those of us who are strong and able in the
    faith need
To step in and lend a hand to those who
    falter,
And not just do what is most convenient for
    us.
Strength is for service, not status.

Joyfully, Joyce

Unity

42

It is important to seek for ways to promote unity in your church. Honor others. Focus on things which you have in common. Let love define your fellowship and relationships. Unity takes effort. It takes positive thinking. It takes humility. You need to be able to overlook faults, weaknesses, imperfections. You need to see that even though we are all imperfect, we are loved perfectly by God.

Ephesians 4:3 states: Endeavor to keep the unity of the Spirit in the bond of peace.

God brings people together to form His church in each area. You need to accept each member as part of God's special family in that location.

Focus on your common love for God. Focus on how God saved each one of us.

Rejoice in the variety and uniqueness that God brings together in the fellowship. The members of the church are like variegated yarn that is knit into a beautiful sweater. Each color enhances the others. Love each member as God's special design.

> I Corinthians 1:10: Be perfectly joined together in the same mind, by the same judgment.

Strengthen your church family by your desire and willingness to be steadfast.

Be true and loyal. Persevere for your church. Build up the body with your prayers.

Show diligence, love, and commitment.

> Romans 14:19 says: Therefore let us pursue the things which make for peace and the things by which one may edify another.

Rejoice in the unity which Jesus prayed for:

That they all may be one, as You, Father, are in Me, and I in You; that they also may be one in Us, That the world may believe that You sent Me. John 17:21

The world will believe in Jesus as they see the unity of Christians.

Joyfully, Joyce

Reconcile

43

God really wants us to get along with each other. The meaning of the word reconcile is: make friendly again, win over, to settle an issue, bring into harmony, make content.

The importance of reconciliation is reflected in the fact that II Corinthians 5:18-20 uses the word 'reconcile' five times. Two times it speaks of the role of God who reconciles us to Himself, and as the One who through Christ is reconciling the world to Himself. Twice, we are spoken of as having the ministry of reconciliation, and the word of reconciliation. Then as ambassadors, God is pleading through us for others to be reconciled to God.

Being reconciled to God leads us to harmony with one another. If there is real value in your relationship with God, then you will live it out with your Christian family. You are encouraged to have the same love, of one accord, of one mind , Philippians 2:1.

As God has freely given you His reconciliation, return the blessing to your brothers and sisters. Keep short accounts with them like you do with God. Learn to resolve differences (reconcile). Practice it. Get good at it. Make it a priority. Value your relationships more than any problem.

Matthew 5:9 states: Blessed are the peacemakers, For they shall be called sons of God.

Learn to dwell on the good, not on the negative. According to Philippians 4:8, your thoughts are to be on the things that are: true, noble, just, pure, lovely, of good report, virtuous, praiseworthy.

I Corinthians 13 states that Love is the key. No spiritual gift is valid of itself. Love is the one absolutely necessary ingredient: it bears all things, believes all things, hopes all things, endures all things. Love never fails.

How far did Christ go for <u>your</u> reconciliation? He went all the way to the cross. II Corinthians 5:21.

Joyfully, Joyce

Follow Me Daily

44

How many times have you heard Christ say, Follow Me. You need to be alert and aware to that call on a daily basis. Your relationship with God is such that you can expect regular communication and contact from your Heavenly Father. Listen carefully.

> Follow Me – first thing in the morning by reading the Word and soaking up Truth and Life.
>
> Follow Me – by turning away from ungodly activities and bad habits.
>
> Follow Me – by stopping to say a kind word or give encouragement to a coworker.

> Follow Me – by taking extra time out of a busy schedule to share love and friendship.
>
> Follow Me – by sharing God's salvation message to a stranger – bringing hope where there was doubt and despair.

The willingness to follow Jesus leads you into unique cooperation with Him, and into wonderful opportunities, and divine appointments. It is a call for a decision, a choice, and an act of the will.

You are called to:

> Put on the Lord Jesus Christ Romans 13:14
>
> Put on the new man, be renewed in the spirit of your mind. Ephesians 4:23
>
> Be transformed by the renewing of your mind. Romans 12:2
>
> Present yourselves as being alive from the dead, and your members as instruments of righteousness to God. Romans 6:13

Be sensitive, listen and you will hear Christ say, Follow Me. Jesus' mother told the servants at the wedding feast, <u>Whatever He says to you, do it.</u> John 2:5 That message is for you as well.

> Follow Me and I will make you fishers of men! Matthew 4:19

Joyfully, Joyce

Trusting In The World

45

Jesus was called The Word. John 1:14 states, the Word became flesh and dwelt among us. Hebrews states that the Word of God is living and powerful, Hebrews 4:12. The Word is truth, John 17:17. My favorite verse on this subject: The entirety of Your Word is truth. Psalm 119:160. How simple to let the Word of God be the measure for truth.

David felt that when he wrote: Forever, O Lord, Your Word is settled in heaven. Psalm 119:89.

Psalms 119 has so much to say about the Word:

Your Word have I hidden in my heart, vs. 11
I will not forget your Word. Vs. 16

> Your Word has given me life. Vs. 50
> Uphold me according to your Word. Vs. 116
> Direct my steps by Your Word. Vs. 133
> Your Word is very pure. Vs. 140
> I rejoice at Your Word. Vs. 162

It is time to make a commitment to accept all of God's Word as truth. Period. Unquestioningly. Completely. If every statement or idea is measured against the truth of the Word, you then have a perfect guide for all of life. God said it. I believe it. That settles it for me.

Each time you read the Word, pray this prayer:

> Open my eyes that I may behold
> Wondrous things out of Your law. Psalm 119:18.

Let the Word be the lamp for your feet and the light for your path.

Joyfully, Joyce

Learning From The Word

46

Oh, send out Your light and Your truth!
Let them lead me Psalm 43:3

Have you ever realized that when you read the Bible, the Word of God, you are receiving messages directly from God? What an awesome opportunity, and an awesome responsibility. If the God of the universe, creator of heaven and earth, is sending you a personalized message, do you think you should pay close attention?

Praise God we have a personal God, who loves each one intimately. He desires to speak to you each day. You have the privilege of reading and benefiting from that message from your Heavenly Father. Reflecting on the Word as you read it each day will help you discern what God is telling you.

There are some simple actions you can take that will help.

- Write down the Scripture verses you read. Such as, Romans 12:1,2
- Summarize the thought in those verses.
- What is the most meaningful thought you read today?
- Reword this thought into a prayer of response to God.
- What does God want you to do in response?

Try this each day for a month. Listen for the ways God speaks to you. Be ready for changes, directions, interaction, challenges, and blessings. At the end of the month, review your notes. Rejoice that the God of the universe has spoken to you and shared His love and concern for your life. Can you see a pattern in the messages God has given you? How will God continue to speak to you in the coming months?

God called the young boy Samuel and he responded: *Speak, for your servant hears.* I Samuel 3:9. When David wrote Psalm 119, he said to the Lord nine times, *Teach me.* He also said, *Revive me in your way. Strengthen me according to Your Word.*

Will you pray the same prayer as Samuel and David?

Joyfully, Joyce

Faith Builders

47

John 16:33 states: In the world you will have
tribulation, but be of good cheer, I have overcome
the world.

Each of the heroes in the Bible was sure of God
and of His presence and plan when they met with
problems.

- Paul and Silas were in prison, but sang
  songs
- Daniel went confidently into the lion's den
- The three Hebrew boys chose to go into
  the fiery furnace.

God used the circumstance s of their lives as a living
testimony of God's greatness. This brought praise and

honor and glory to God. Joseph, who was sold into slavery and spent years in prison, told his brothers that God meant it for good, and God's purpose was fulfilled.

The men in the Bible believed they were in the center of God's will. They believed God led them. They believed that God was with them. Thus they believed their circumstances were God-anointed.

Expect that God will give you faith-building experiences. In the dark, the only thing you can believe is the greatness of His love and purpose. The only One you can turn to is the Father. Expect that your faith after the trial will be stronger then before. Expect that more glory and praise will go to God as a result of the trial. God is in the business of building your faith.

> Rejoice always. Pray without ceasing. In everything give thanks for this is the will of God for you. I Thessalonians 5:16-18

Trust God to lead you through the most difficult circumstances of life. Trust that He is building your faith-walk. Allow Him to receive the glory and the praise for victory.

Joyfully, Joyce

Victory Over Temptations

48

Wouldn't you love it if you didn't have to deal with temptations any more. Maybe you wish you could just find one prayer and they would all be gone. However, that is not reality. God knows you will deal with temptation every day. There is always going to be a struggle, a war, a place where Satan will try to pull you away from God and separate you from your mission.

The devil moves about like a roaring lion seeking whom he may devour, I Peter 5:8. But you are told in James 4:7 to resist the devil and he will flee from you. The devil knows your weaknesses. You can be pulled away by your own desires. He will try to deceive you and cause you to stumble. Look at the passage in James

4:7-10 to find the guidance you need. In this passage there are added ways to resist him.

- Submit to God
- Resist the devil
- Cleanse your hands (repent)
- Purify your heart (confess)
- Lament and mourn and weep (grieve)
- Humble yourselves in the sight of the Lord.

God gives you the tools to daily stand firm. You are told to think on what is:

> true, noble, just, pure, lovely, of good report, what is of virtue, and worthy of praise Philippians 4:8

Commit your mind to God. Seek His way. Where can you find more of what is good, but in the Word! So fill your mind with the Word of God.

> Psalm 119:15 I will meditate on your precepts, I will contemplate Your ways, I will delight myself in your statutes, I will not forget Your word.

Joyfully, Joyce

Daily Preparations

49

Ephesians 6: 10-18 urges you to put on the full armor of God. Be equipped, ready for battle. The more successful you are in serving God, the bigger target you are for Satan to attack. You must dress properly for battle each day.

> Belt: Truth
> Breastplate: Righteousness
> Shoes: Preparation of the Gospel
> Shield: Faith
> Helmet: Salvation
> Sword: Word of God

You have two orders to follow: Stand and Pray.

The MESSAGE translation puts it this way:

> Be prepared. You are up against far more than you can handle on your own. Take all the help you can get, every weapon God has issued, so that when it is all over but the shouting you will still be on your feet.

> Your full armor of protection is needed to stand and withstand. You are encouraged to: pray hard and long. Pray for all your brothers and sisters, too. Keep your eyes open. Keep each other's spirits up so that no one falls behind or drops out.

The Message 6:12, 13, 18

Your marching orders do not say IF the enemy comes, but WHEN the enemy comes. You are only safe when you are wearing truth, righteousness, preparation of the Gospel, faith, salvation and the Word of God.

Joyfully, Joyce

Experience God's Provision

50

Have you ever thought about how these verses go together:

Matthew 6:33
>   Seek first the kingdom of God and His righteousness
>   And all these things shall be added unto you.

Philippians 4:19
>   But my God shall supply all your needs according to
>   His riches in glory by Christ Jesus

Matthew 7:7

> Ask and it will be given to you
> Seek and you will find
> Knock and it will be opened to you.

First, you need to have your priorities straight. You must put first things first: the things of God. Kingdom things. This takes focus, determination, and a decision to do it all in the way God would have you do it. It takes time for you to relinquish your will to God and to His will. At times it takes opening up your hands to God and say to Him, 'whatever, Lord.'

Next, comes expectation. Paul expected God to supply all their needs. You can expect that, too. And that supply is not limited by your resources. It is a provision according to His riches! Your Father is able to do:

> Exceedingly abundantly above all that you ask or think, according to the Power that works in you. Ephesians 3:20

Finally, you are told to Ask, Seek, and Knock. That is pro-active, it is diligent, it is persistent. It is WORK! That type of action continues, because it knows God has the answer.

Are you willing to apply this type of Kingdom Power to a big problem today? Please keep a record of your needs and the miraculous way God answers. That is your testimony of God keeping His word in your life. I look forward to hearing some mighty answers from you about our Mighty God. We will rejoice together.

Philippians 4:20 ends by saying:

Now to our God and Father be glory forever and ever. Amen

Joyfully, Joyce

He Is Always There

51

How often we take the promises of God so lightly. He says He will keep you in the shadow of His hand. He says that He is your Rock, your Fortress and your Deliverer. (Psalm 18:1-3) He says He will protect you and be your Shield. He says He will answer when you call to Him. (Psalm 91:15) You may accept all of these promises right now. Meditate on them. Tuck them away in your memory until the crisis comes.

The crisis may be physical, emotional or financial. There is also a spiritual battleground. It is at that time that you can claim the promises of God. You can call out His name when you are desperate. You can hide in the cleft of the Rock, and behind the Shield of protection. You can call on Him and be sure that He will hear and answer you. You will not be left alone, for He will never leave you or forsake you. (Hebrews 13:5) When you are in the storm and in the dark, there is new meaning and dimension to the promises God gives in Psalm 18:1-3; Psalm 46:1-3 and Isaiah 43:1,2. God IS a very present help in trouble. God knows your name.

Your journey is not to be taken alone. Many are there along the way to help and pray and give you encouragement. In turn, you will be helping others as they go through their struggles. The truth is, we all need help from our Father and also from our brothers and sisters in Christ.

Thank your Father that He hears and answers your prayers. The crisis will pass. Thank Him for going through the valley with you. Thank Him for miracles. Thank Him for comfort and healing. And thank Him for those who are there to help when you cry out to Him.

> He who dwells in the secret place of the Most High, shall abide under the shadow of the Almighty. Psalm 91:1

Joyfully, Joyce

Growing In God's Family

52

Do you remember as a small child how you thought everything would be great when you grew up? When you grow up, you can go to school. When you grow up, you can ride a bicycle. When you grow up you can go to high school. When you grow up you can drive a car. And on it goes. There are always things in the future that are just out of reach, things you will really like to do or be.

The same is true in Gods kingdom. You may long to grow and be a seasoned Christian. You may think things will be a whole lot easier when you just grow a little longer in Gods family. You are in a hurry to get there. You may look with longing at leaders and teachers and counselors and desire to know the Word just like them.

Have you ever tasted fruit that was not yet ripe? It can be pretty sour, not sweet and tasty. The same is true of your Christian life. It is best to allow time to grow and let the love of God take root in your life. Let it feed and nourish you thoroughly on a daily basis. Let the time spent in the Word give you wisdom and understanding. Much of what God is teaching you is going to be spread over a lifetime. God is in for the long haul, and will be with you every day of your life, guiding and nurturing you. Relax and enjoy the journey.

I encourage you to record what God is teaching you each day as you read the Word and trust God more. Review the lessons and answers to prayer.

Growing in Gods kingdom is a life journey. That is what your church is for. Your church helps to guide you, direct you, counsel you, comfort and protect you.

Ephesians 4:13-15 states

> till we all come to the unity of the faith and
> of the knowledge
> of the Son of God, to a perfect man, to the
> measure of the stature
> of the fullness of Christ… but speaking the
> truth in love, may

grow up in all things into Him who is the head – Christ…

When I grow up, I want to be just like Jesus…one day at a time!

Joyfully, Joyce

Being Properly Dressed

53

It is always nice to know that God is specific in His directions, even down to what He wants you to wear! Are you surprised? God is always looking out for your best interests, and what you wear and how you present yourself is of utmost importance. Of course you know you are representing the Company – that is heaven. So putting your best foot forward and making a good first impression is important. You are the first representative, or ambassador that many people meet. If any of these items are missing in your attire, it will be noticed immediately and have an adverse effect. The stakes are high in adding new members to the company. A well-dressed representative always draws attention to the heavenly country.

Here is the list, in Colossians 3:12-17

> And so, as those who have been chosen of God, holy and dearly loved, clothe your-selves with compassion, kindness, humility, gentleness and patience,

> bearing with one another and forgiving each other…just as the Lord forgave you, so also should you.

> And beyond all these things put on love, which is the perfect bond of unity.

Check your wardrobe. Make sure nothing is missing. Reflect on the Word and let it help you put on the best clothes for the job. You are an ambassa-dor of God, the Lord of heaven and earth. Let Him be proud of your appearance.

COMPASSION
KINDNESS
HUMILITY
GENTLENESS
PATIENCE
FORGIVENESS
LOVE

Joyfully, Joyce

For Such A Time As This

54

Perhaps you have read the story of Esther. She was orphaned and raised by an uncle. Her people were ruled by another country. When the king of the country was looking for the most beautiful woman in the realm to become his new wife, she was a candidate and finally the one chosen to be queen.

However, there were evil men in the King's court who plotted against her uncle and against her people, to have them all killed. Her uncle appealed to Esther to help save the people by pleading with the King. This was risky, because if a person was not personally invited by the King but came to him unannounced, that one could be killed.

Esther's uncle told her this was the only way to save her people, and he said that perhaps she had become queen for such a time as this. Esther bravely took the challenge and appeared before the King. He accepted her presence and she was able to intercede for her people and save them from death.

Can you view your role in being placed where you are, sharing what you know, and being the one to speak out, for such a time as this? What is your purpose? How will you fulfill your goal?

Like Esther, this is risky business. Like Esther, you could face harmful consequences. But like Esther, you have the words that can help people find new life with the Father, the one true God. Perhaps you were brought to this place for such a time as this.

What a privilege to be used to give such good news to hungry people.

A familiar hymn says,
> Sing them over again to me
> Wonderful words of life
> Let me more of their beauty see

Words of life and beauty
Teach me faith and duty
Beautiful words, Wonderful words,
Wonderful words of life.

Joyfully, Joyce

Healthy Plants

55

Organic fruit and vegetables are thought to be the best tasting and the most nourishing. They are vine-ripened. They have had plenty of rich soil and the right amounts of sun and water to grow to be the very best. They are vitamin rich. They are juicy, full-flavored, and succulent.

You should seek to be an 'organic Christian.' You need to draw full nourishment regularly from the Word. Soak up all that can enrich you and help you mature. God designs just the right amount of sun and rain and nutrients, and, yes, just the right amount of fertilizer, for you to grow. God personally allots the perfect amount for your individual growth regimen. This helps you develop the fruit that God has designed for your ministry.

Your church family is an important factor in your growth and development. This is the farmland where God planted you. The family is designed for each member to become:

> a perfect man, to the measure of the stature of the fullness of Christ. Ephesians 4:13

Let the fruit of the Spirit become well-established habits in your life. Let these habits define your character. Let each fruit bloom like a strong, healthy plant:

> Love, joy, peace, longsuffering, kindness, goodness, faithfulness, gentleness, and self-control. Galatians 5:22

Let the character of God grow slowly, deeply in your spirit, not picked prematurely, but aged to perfection, warmed by the light of His encouraging love.

Joyfully, Joyce

Born To Serve

56

God has called each of us to follow in His footsteps. Those footsteps lead us down the path of service. He stated in Matthew 20: 27, 28

> Whoever desires to be first among you, let him be your slave, just as the Son of Man did not come to be served but to serve, and to give His life a ransom for many.

You have the privilege of also living to serve. You are here to meet the needs of others, and let the rivers of the Living Water flow through you. Therein is the passion of the Christian life. Just as Jesus did exactly as He saw the Father doing, so we are to do exactly what we see Jesus do. You become the eyes, the ears, the hands, the heart of the church and of the Father. You become the message that can be accepted and understood by the many.

Jesus did not shy away from serving. When He was tired, or mourning, or frustrated by religious leaders, still He had time to stop and heal the blind man, help the hurting woman, hug the children, sit down and share His message, and feed the multitudes. You are saved to serve. You are called to serve under every circumstance. Serving others gives you permission to share the message of salvation. It is then you can deliver the message of Hope to a hurting world.

> Galatians 6:9 And let us not grow weary while doing good, for in due season we shall reap if we do not lose heart.

This is the key to a peaceful, happy, joyful life: serve others. It is God's way.

Joyfully, Joyce

God Made You

57

Many people would like to change their appearance – too tall, too short, too thin, too fat, not the right facial features. Others are troubled or ashamed of their past: too poor, too hurt, dysfunctional family, and many more skeletons!

Romans 8:28 states:
> And we know that all things work together for good to those who love God, to those who are the called according to His purpose.

Amazingly enough, God accepts you and uses you just as you are. You are exactly the person to minister in the places and to the people God chooses. There are no mistakes in your past, present or future that God will not use to His glory if you give them to Him and praise Him for how He designed you. Wow! What a thought!

Ephesians 2:10 says:
> For we are His workmanship created in Christ Jesus for good works which God prepared beforehand that we should walk in them.

That is why you are called a light in this world. People are drawn to the light. The light in you is Jesus Christ. As others come to you, they are drawn to Jesus.

Joyfully, Joyce

Holy DNA

58

Isn't it amazing how God made each person different. We are just now learning the miracle of DNA that God used to make you so special. You are definitely a one of a kind design. You are God's chosen vessel for this place and this time. No one else is in the position you are and has the circle of influence you have to speak for the Father. All of your gifts and abilities and past experiences are part of the package that proves God's amazing love.

As a Christian, God has appointed you and anointed you in service to share His love right where you are. You are God's message to a world longing for answers.

For we are His workmanship, created in Christ Jesus to do good works, which God prepared beforehand that we should walk in them. Ephesians 2:10

Let your light so shine before men that they may see your good works and glorify your Father in heaven.

Matthew 5:16

As you read the Word daily, God speaks to you the words of love that you are privileged to share with others. Rise! Shine! Give God the glory!

Whatever you do, do all to the glory of God.
II Corinthians 10:17

Joyfully, Joyce

Be All That You Can Be

59

The army has this motto that exemplifies your daily walk. God has given you certain abilities, wonderful spiritual gifts and some unbelievable life experiences all bundled up into one person. You can believe that He has gifted you to use it all to honor Him.

He wants you to be
> Always abounding in the work of the Lord.
> For you know your labor is not in vain in the Lord. I Cor. 15:58

You are part of God's holy army, ready and on call for service. The Holy Spirit speaks to you. You are to be willing to obey orders. You are well-prepared with holy armor (Ephesians 6) and a powerful Sword. You take your stand against the enemy, but there is more for you to do.

The hungry and hurting are all around you crying out for help, for comfort. They need the Good News. You have the words of salvation. You have the Spirit of power and you have the strength to do all things through Him. Therefore, use it all wisely. Be willing to share. Let the love of Christ flow through you. Be all that you can be.

Joyfully, Joyce

Being A Servant

60

If you follow Christ's example, you will choose to take the role of a servant. Jesus humbled himself in every way and God exalted Him. Philippians 2:5-11. Jesus washed feet. Jesus touched lepers. Jesus kept company with sinners. Jesus was not politically correct.

There is a chorus which states:

> Make me a servant, humble and meek
> Lord may I lift up those who are weak
> And may the theme of my song always be
> Make me a servant today.

This is a choice. It is a gift back to God. Just as Jesus had a choice, you can follow in His steps. You can make that sacrifice, too.

> Hebrews 13:16 But do not forget to do good, for with such sacrifices God is well pleased.

Whatever your job or position, whoever the people are in your circle, commit to be a servant. Do it privately, silently. Let the Lord reward you. Open your eyes to the possibilities. Serve the helpless. Entertain those who cannot return the favor.

Ask God, how can I be a servant today? How will I let the love of Jesus flow through me?

> Matthew 25:40 says, Assuredly I say to you, inasmuch as you did it to one of the least of these My brethren, you did it to Me.

Joyfully, Joyce

Making A Choice

61

Joshua made his choice when he spoke to all of the Israelites. He said:

> As for me and my house we will serve the Lord. Joshua 24:15

When you choose to serve the Lord you are empowered by the Holy Spirit. You are given direction. You choose to accept God's plan for your life.

This simplifies everything and at the same time it makes life exciting. You can ask: Lord, where would you have me to share with others today?

God gives you gifts – to each one according to their abilities. Accept the gifts God gives to you. Use them fully. Allow the Holy Spirit to give you power. All God asks is that you be available to do His work. You are called upon to be diligent, responsible and work with integrity.

It all centers around choice: choosing to serve the Lord. Choosing to accept the gifts. Choosing to use the gifts for the glory of God.

David wrote passionately about it: Psalm 84:10

> For a day in Your courts is better than a thousand I would rather be a doorkeeper in the house of my God than to dwell in the tents of wickedness.

The choice is yours. The rewards are eternal.

Joyfully, Joyce

By My Spirit Zechariah 4:6

62

So many of the principles God uses are the opposite of our thinking. He says be humble in order to be great. He says you must die to self in order to really live. You may think: My weakness keeps me from serving God. You may be frustrated because your weakness may seem like it is in the way of serving God. Please think again.

You cannot change your past – the pain, the traumas, the disappointments, the bad mistakes. But God promises to use them for His glory if you say YES to Him. Being weak is not a problem with God. In fact, that is the very type of person God uses to serve.

> But God has chosen the foolish things of the world to put to shame the wise, and God has chosen the weak things of the world to put to shame the things which are mighty. I Corinthians 1:27-29

Your weakness is actually an advantage with God. God says, your weakness shows God's strength and gives Him glory. How awesome! Paul was troubled by his physical problem and pleaded with God to take it away. Instead, he learned a Spirit-filled principle:

> And He said to me, My grace is sufficient for you, for My strength is made perfect in weakness. Therefore most gladly I will rather boast in my infirmities, that the power of Christ may rest upon me. II Corinthians 12:9

Will you depend on the power of God and the filling of the Holy Spirit to accomplish His mission? Then God gets the glory, and we are blessed.

> Not by might, nor by power, but by My Spirit, says the Lord of Hosts. Zechariah 4:6

Joyfully, Joyce

Ministry And Mission

63

The Bible teaches that all Christians are to have ministry with their brothers and sisters. That ministry is to encourage, mentor, teach, disciple, pray, lift up spiritually, edify those who are a part of our church family. Look to see those around you that you can bless with ministry. All of the gifts which the Spirit gives are to be used to strengthen the family members.

> Till we all come to the unity of the faith and of the knowledge of the Son of God, to a perfect man, to the measure of the stature of the fullness of Christ. Ephesians 4:13

Also, we are all ambassadors, representatives, deliverers of Good News, agents, partners, co-laborers, missionaries, "small-a apostles" (messengers) to those who have not yet come to know God's amazing Love.

Do not be discouraged with the task ahead of you. All that is asked of you is that you present yourself as an instrument of righteousness. God will do the rest through you.

> Romans 6:13 …but present yourselves to God as being alive from the dead, and your members as instruments of righteousness to God.

Do not rely on your own strength or ability, but rely on the power of the Holy Spirit. God gives you the ministry. God presents the task. And God provides the strength to accomplish it.

My challenge for you: Who will you see in heaven because you shared the Gospel? Who will you see in heaven that you prayed for and encouraged in the Word? Become an instrument of righteousness that will bless others.

Joyfully, Joyce

Sharing Your Faith

64

Have you thought about how wonderful it is to be able to let others know about the faith that you have? This is a privilege. This is your calling. At each opportunity you again get to review what God has done in a personal, intimate way to lead you to Him. Paul shared his testimony two times in Acts, after the event was recorded. How many times do you think he shared his story on his travels?

I Peter 3:15 states you are
> always to be ready to give a defense to everyone who asks you for the hope that is in you with meekness and fear.

Every testimony simply told, will have an effect

on those who hear it. It is the Holy Spirit speaking to those around you. It does not have to be long or elaborate.

Focus on your message. Be proactive. Be prepared. Your message is unique, it is original. It needs to be shared honestly, and with the passion and love that God has given you. You need to work on this, write it down. Let the information flow.

All you need to do is answer three simple questions:
1. What was your life before you met Christ?
2. How did you come to accept Christ?
3. How has your life changed since meeting Christ?

Keep your facts short and simple. Find Bible the verses that helped you to understand the Gospel. Find an easy Gospel Tract that you can use to share the message.

It is so wonderful to see what impact your personal experience can have on others. The Holy Spirit works through your words. He confirms the love that God has for the whole world. Let God's love for the world excite you and energize you.

God bless you as you work on this adventure of partnership with the Father.

Joyfully, Joyce

Life Lessons

65

Life lessons are those wonderful insights God teaches you personally. As you are walking with Him, and you go through trials and hard times, God gives you insights you did not have before. You are experiencing His love and care and protection, His peace and joy through the storms of life.

Reflect on the different stages of your life and write down the lessons God has taught you through those times. Your difficulties are not lost experiences, but they hold treasures of wisdom shared with you by a loving Father.

He said: I will never leave you or forsake you. Hebrews 13:5

He said: He shall call upon Me, and I will answer him. I will be with him in trouble. Psalm 91:15

He said: In all your ways acknowledge Me and I will direct your ways. Proverbs 3:6

What did God teach you in your teen years? What did He teach you as a single adult? What did God teach you through your career choice? What did God teach you through sorrow, pain, trauma, loss and disappointment? What Scripture has special meaning because God gave it to you at just the right time?

What are the life lessons that you have been given? Those are lessons that you are able to share with others. They are personal, intimate encounters with the Father. They are ministry and encouragement for others. Write them down. Pass them on.

Pray that you can share your life lessons with others.

Joyfully, Joyce

Share The Message

66

What a privilege it is to share good news. Learn to love people because God loves them. Let them know the message of His love. Simply. Unconditionally. Be willing to learn to share. You have the best news of all.

A messenger is one who delivers important information. The messenger is responsible ONLY to deliver the news. When you have good news to share, there is excitement, joy, enthusiasm. Be bursting with the news.

Start now to find a plan that is easy, comfortable for you, just enough to tell the Story. Use it over and over as you find those who want to hear. Make this your life goal. God will provide the opportunities. They are called Divine Appointments.

The Holy Spirit reaches the hearts of those listening and wanting to know.

Man sins – Romans 3:23
God loves – John 3:16
Jesus paid – I Peter 2:24
Man repents – Acts 2:38
Grace saves – Ephesians 2:8
Sins forgiven – Ephesians 1:7
Gift received – John 1:12
Go to heaven – John 3:16, Romans 6:23

I urge you to take this seriously. Be diligent, fervent, compelled, ready, and intentional with your desire to share the news.

Gloria Gaither wrote these words several years ago:

Because He lives I can face tomorrow
Because He lives all fear is gone
Because I know He holds the future
And life is worth the living just because He lives.

Share the message.

Joyfully, Joyce

Prayer Partners

67

Paul the great missionary understood the power prayer. He knew he needed prayer warriors to intercede for him. The church in Antioch sent him out with prayer.

He asked for the Christians in Rome:
Romans 15:30 ...that you strive together with me in prayers to God for me, that I may be delivered from those in Judea who do not believe, and that my service for Jerusalem may be acceptable to the saints, that I may come to you with joy by the will of God...

Paul asked the Ephesians:
Ephesians 6:18, 19 ...and (pray) for me, that

utterance may be given to me, that I may open my mouth boldly to make known the mystery of the gospel…that in it I may speak boldly, as I ought to speak.

He wrote to the Thessalonians:

II Thes. 3:1 pray that the word of the Lord may run swiftly and be glorified … and that we may be delivered from unreasonable and wicked men.

As a Christian you need to follow Paul's example. Having prayer partners and prayer warriors is not an option but a necessity. God leads you to serve Him as a link in a chain, and the other links are those who are praying for you. Share your needs and your struggles with faithful Christians who will be diligent to pray.

James says: that we need to confess our sins one to another that we may be healed.

James 5:16 Confess your trespasses to one another and pray for one another that you may be healed.

The effectual, fervent prayer of a righteous man avails much.

It is humbling but good to be transparent enough to share personal needs with those you trust to pray. Having a mentor, a partner, a close friend in the Lord who will drop everything in order to pray for you, can lift the heavy burden you are carrying. Ask for protection from the enemy. Ask for courage and strength. Ask for boldness in sharing the Message.

Joyfully, Joyce

Take A Good Look

68

You are important in God's kingdom. You have value, position and purpose. God has placed you at this location and at this particular time in history to be His light to the world and His encourager to your fellow Christians.

I want to encourage you to reserve time in your busy schedule for a spiritual check-up. Set aside a block of time in your date book for this important review. Use this special time to reflect on where God has led you and what He has taught you. It is good to measure progress.

Look at your life as stages, sections of growth and service.

- What significant things have happened in the past year? How have people you have met influenced your walk with Jesus?
- In the past five years, what lessons has God taught you in difficult situations. What verses has God given you to cling to during your walk with Him?
- How has God revealed Himself personally? Which part of the Bible blessed you with courage to meet the challenge?

Once you have reflected on life lessons, write down what you have learned. You are then able to share your experiences with others. The blessings you have received are also passed on to others. In fact, God may have plans for Christians in years to come to be encouraged by your documented walk with the Lord.

Psalm 102:18 states that
> These are written down so generations to come may praise the Lord.

Understanding that your Heavenly Father loves you dearly and has brought you so far, gives new hope for the future. It is exciting to wonder

what new encounters and experiences God has
in store for you, as He continues to reveal His
love.

Joyfully, Joyce

A Life Purpose Statement

69

I encourage you to take time to pray and meditate on the Word this week. Seek God to help you write a purpose statement for your life. A purpose statement gives you a goal, a direction, a guideline for your life. It defines where you are going so you can plan how to get there. It is there to keep you on track. It helps you stay focused. It lets you know if you stray. Each new opportunity, challenge, work, relationship and major change can then be measured by your Life Purpose Statement. Ask God to give you a Life Verse. This will take time, but will be well worth the effort.

Pastor Rick Warren wrote a book called <u>The Purpose Driven Life</u> which discusses the five essentials of purpose for life: Decide who will be at the <u>center</u> of your life. Determine what will define your <u>character</u>. Visualize what will be your <u>contribution</u>. Decide what you will <u>communicate</u> with your life. Finally, consider what <u>community</u> you desire to serve with your life.

Paul says:

> ...forgetting those things which are behind and reaching forward to those things which are ahead, I press toward the goal for the prize of the upward call of God in Christ Jesus.

At the end of His life on earth, Jesus said:

> I have finished the work which You have given me to do. John 17:4

Paul states:

> I have fought the good fight, I have finished the race. II Timothy 4:7

Your life is like a flower: The leaves and blooms reach up to the heavens. The roots go down deep in the soil for nourishment. The flower turns toward the light. The flower blooms where it is planted. Finally, the plant is a part of a great garden.

Joyfully, Joyce

Devotion On Grieving

70

When you are grieving, there is great comfort in going to the Word of God. Read the promises over and over. Let the message sink into your heart. When you cry out to the Father, you are touching the very heart of God. God understands your sorrows and grief. He does not minimize the time for grieving. Jesus is 'a man of sorrows and acquainted with grief.' (Isaiah 53:6) Jesus wept as he saw the mourning of Mary and Martha when their brother Lazarus died. (John 11:35)

Psalm 56:8 states that God has a record of every tear you shed. They are all precious to him. God is with you always. He says,

'I will never leave you or forsake you, so we

can boldly say, 'The Lord is my helper, I shall never fear.' (Hebrews 13:5, 6)

You can look to God our Father as your personal Shepherd. (Psalm 23) He directs and guides your steps. Jesus calls you to come to Him when you are weary and heavy laden and He will give you rest. With Him you will find rest for your soul. (Matthew 11:29,30)

God so loved you that He sacrificed His only begotten Son. (John 3:16) You are that important to Him. God is our refuge and strength, a very present help in trouble. (Psalm 46:1) God will walk with you through the valley. (Psalm 23) Lean on Him for strength and comfort.

You have a time for mourning, weeping and grieving, but God promises you that He will bring you through it to a new day. Jesus has come to:
> Heal the brokenhearted
> Proclaim liberty to the captives
> To open the prison of those who are bound
> To comfort all who mourn. Isaiah 61:1

You are encouraged to offer Him a sacrifice of praise. When your heart is broken, your praise to

God is a sacrifice. You are to add to that the sacrifices of doing good and sharing. This pleases God. (Hebrews 13:15, 16) God will use these gifts and bless you as you reach out through your sorrow. He will exchange:

> Beauty for ashes
> The oil of joy for mourning
> The garment of praise for the spirit of heaviness. Isaiah 61:3

This is a promise to cling to. This is the hope you have. Weeping may endure for the night but joy comes in the morning. (Psalm 30:5).

> Trust in the Lord with all your heart
> And lean not on your own understanding
> In all your ways acknowledge Him
> And He shall direct your paths. Proverbs 3:5

Joyfully, Joyce

Who Is Jesus?

71

The Bible shares the wonderful news of just who Jesus is. Rest assured God says you can know the truth through His Word. Many people have asked and searched and wondered. Consider now what the Bible says about who Jesus is:

- He is the image of the invisible God Col. 1:15
- He is the WORD John 1:14
- He is the brightness of God's glory Hebrews 1:3
- He is the express image of God's person Hebrews 1:3
- He is Heir of all things Hebrews 1:1

- In Him dwells all the fullness of the Godhead bodily Col. 2:9
- He is the Light of the World John 8:12
- He is the promised Messiah John 1:41
- He is the humble Savior who gave up everything to save us Phil. 2:7
- He paid the penalty for all our sins. Hebrews 1:3, I Peter 2:24
- He is King of Kings and Lord of Lords I Tim 6:15
- He is seated at the right hand of the Majesty on high Hebrews 1:3

Once you know the truth, you are able to reach out and praise Him, give Him Glory. Your communication with Him will give you joy, peace, overflowing love – victory through every difficulty.

Take time to meditate and pray over these verses. Look to see who Jesus is in your own heart and life. Allow the verses to open your innermost being to Him.

All honor, praise, glory be to Him who loves us so much.

Joyfully, Joyce

Trusting God

72

Has fear ever been a problem for you? Often life may hand you issues you cannot solve on your own. They may appear to be overwhelming and insurmountable! Fear comes when you try to predict the future in the light of the problems you face. The enemy, (Satan) wants to defeat you with fear.

The Bible speaks about how to handle fear.

Psalm 91:1 "He who dwells in the secret place of the Most High shall abide under the shadow of the Almighty."

Psalm 18: 1, 2 "I will bless you oh God, my strength. The Lord is my rock and my fortress and my Deliverer, my God my strength in whom I will trust, my Shield and the horn of my salvation, my Stronghold. I will call upon the Lord who is worthy to be praised. So shall I be saved from my enemies."

Psalm 23: Yea though I walk through the valley of the shadow of death, I will fear no evil for You are with me."

Is that the safe place where you would like to be? God says it is your privilege to be there. You have the right to be there where God can answer your problems and deal with your enemies. God wants to shelter you and protect you. You can speak these verses out loud every time fear comes knocking at your door. They will give you assurance, confidence and peace.

So many times in the Bible you are told "Fear not, do not be afraid."

Joshua 1:9 "Be strong and of good courage; do not be afraid, nor dismayed, for the Lord your God is with you wherever you go."

Here are some other verses to consider that will help you.

"God is love… Perfect love casts out fear." I John 4:16, 18

"God has not given us a spirit of fear, but of power and of love and of a sound mind." II Timothy 1:7

Coming to God, repenting of sin, asking forgiveness, brings you back into fellowship with Him. You can have protection and help in all the troubles of life. You can know that He will work out the details of your life and bring you into the blessings He has promised. God knows the future! God loves you! You are His special creation.

Trust in God today!

Joyfully, Joyce

The Word

73

We are so blessed today to have the Word of God, the Bible, to lead us and teach us in all righteousness. The Bible is available in our community, and you can find a translation that helps you understand.

Be sure to use the word daily, read it, absorb it, study it, meditate on it. Reading the Bible does not need to be a marathon. You are not always on a time schedule to see how many chapters you can read at a time. Yes, you will be blessed as you read the whole Bible. However, verse by verse, the Holy Spirit teaches, blesses, and encourages Christians. That is your privilege as a Christian. Some days, a few verses will be what you need to grow and be blessed.

The Bible states in II Timothy 3:16:

> "All scripture is given by inspiration of God and is profitable for doctrine, for reproof, for correction and for instruction in righteousness."

II Timothy 2:15

> "Study to show yourself approved unto God, a workman that need not be ashamed, rightly dividing the word of truth."

God wants you to be diligent to study and accept what is written in the Bible. You are to use it for the intended purpose of being taught and making the right changes of action to grow as a faithful follower of Christ.

David spoke of the word of the Lord as a lamp for your feet and a light for your path. (Psalm 119:105) Memorizing and meditating on the word keeps you from sin and leads you into a life in tune with God. (Psalm 119:9,11; Joshua 1:8)

Colossians 3:16 encourages,

> "Let the word of Christ dwell in you richly."

Allow God to speak to you daily through the

Word. Allow the Holy Spirit to open your eyes to new truths and lead you into a closer relationship with your Father.

Joyfully, Joyce

Guidelines For Christians

74

It is helpful to have a checklist for personal growth as a Christian. This helps you to see where you are going and how to make the next steps. I found some suggestions while studying in the book of Romans that gives you just such guidelines.

	Romans 12: 9-16
LOVE	Let love be without hypocrisy
	Abhor what is evil. Cling to what is good.
OTHERS	Be kindly affectionate to one another with brotherly love
	In honor, giving preference to one another;

WORK	Not lagging in diligence Fervent in spirit Serving the Lord;
OUTLOOK	Rejoicing in hope Patient in tribulation Continuing steadfastly in prayer;
CARE	Distributing to the needs of the saints, Given to hospitality.
REACT	Bless those who persecute you Bless and do not curse.
RELATE	Rejoice with those who rejoice Weep with those who weep.
SHARE	Be of the same mind toward one another. Do not set your mind on high things But associate with the humble.
SELF	Do not be wise in your own opinion.

Thank the Lord for giving you such focused directions for Godly living.

Joyfully, Joyce

You Are Special

75

It is important to know who you are in God's eyes. God wants you to see your worth, your value, so He has written a love letter to you called the Bible. When you fill your thoughts with the truth God gives, you have an image of a very special person. YOU!

God tells you there:

> I love you – John 3:16
> I know you by your name - Isaiah 43:1
> I sing over you – Zephaniah 3:17
> I am with you always Matthew 28:20
> I want to adopt you. Ephesians 1:5
> I sent my Son to die for you. John 3:16

I have plans to give you a future and a hope.
Jeremiah 29:17
I am preparing a home for you. John 14:1

The paradox God tells you is, if you want to gain your life, you need to lose it. God is the One who gives you value, purpose, direction and importance. He gives it His way. When you give yourself to God, sharing your time, purpose, career, and effort, you will find life and purpose. Your example is Jesus. Jesus served others, even though He is the King of Kings! Jesus washed the feet of the disciples to show them an example of serving. He touched the leper and healed him. He spoke to a Samaritan woman and gave Her hope.

Pour yourself out, give your time, your effort, your talents. Focus on others and their needs. Commit yourself passionately to a cause. God promises that the more you give, the more will come back to you.

Luke 6:38 Give and it shall be given to you, pressed down, shaken together and running over will be put into your bosom. For with the same measure you use, it will be measured back to you.

God says we can test Him and see if He will not open the windows of heaven in blessings so there will not be room to receive it. Malachi 3:10

Are you willing to try life God's way?

Joyfully, Joyce

Character

76

You say your desire is to be more like Jesus. God hears and answers that prayer. The answer to your prayer may not exactly be what you were expecting. However, James 1:2 tells you to count it all joy because the end result is worth the effort.

In Ephesians 4:22-25 you are called to:
>Put off – the old man
>Put on – the new man
>Put away – the old behavior

All of this is accomplished by submitting to the work of the Holy Spirit in your life.

A rock is hard and coarse, but with constant sand-ing it becomes smooth and shiny. Life circumstances are the sandpaper God uses to polish your character until you shine and reflect Jesus! The old rock has no ability to shine or reflect. The newly polished rock reflects light beautifully. Your witness shines in the midst of the difficult times you experience.

Romans 12:2 states:

> Do not be conformed to this world But be transformed by the renewing of your mind… that you may prove what is that good and acceptable and perfect will of God.

God uses all of your life challenges to develop your character, and to let you know how much you can trust Him and how much He loves you. This is the testimony that draws others to follow Jesus. This is your life witness. This is your ministry. Rejoice in what God gives you.

Joyfully, Joyce

Breinigsville, PA USA
16 December 2009
229380BV00001B/21/P